# LITURGY & LIFE

## — Unveiling the —

## MYSTICAL MOVEMENT *of the* MASS

## SCIENCE *of* SAINTHOOD

# SCIENCE *of* SAINTHOOD

*Nihil Obstat:*
The Reverend James M. Dunfee, MA, STL
Censor Librorum
May 12, 2025

*Imprimatur:*
The Most Reverend Edward M. Lohse, JCD
Apostolic Administrator of Steubenville
May 14, 2025

The *nihil obstat* and *imprimatur* do not signify agreement with the content, opinions, or statements expressed but simply affirm that the content does not contradict faith and morals.

Video Study Written by Matthew Leonard

Workbook Written by Matthew Leonard & John Paul Nunez

Workbook Edited by Curtis Mitch

Cover Design and layout by Patty Borgman

**Science Of Sainthood | ScienceOfSainthood.com**

# Table of Contents

# Welcome to the Science of Sainthood

Welcome to *Liturgy & Life: Unveiling the Mystical Movement of the Mass*, presented by the Science of Sainthood.

Founded by evangelist Matthew Leonard, the Science of Sainthood is one of the world's premier online Catholic platforms dedicated to teaching authentic Catholic spirituality. Steeped in the tradition of Saints like John of the Cross, Teresa of Avila, and Thomas Aquinas, our goal is to guide regular Catholics, step by step, down the path to nothing less than sainthood.

More than education, this is *transformation*!

# How to Use This Workbook

This study is just one of many powerful courses on Catholic spirituality you'll find at ScienceOfSainthood.com. Visit the site to learn more.

Each lesson in this study contains the following sections:

* Short Introduction
* Review of the Previous Lesson
* Lesson Video
* Space to Take Notes on the Video Lesson
* A Passage from a Saint
* A Passage from Sacred Scripture for Lectio Divina
* Written Meditation
* Review & Discussion Questions
* Prayer Journal

How you use the sections depends completely on what works best for you and/or your group. The written sections are there for either group or individual use. Some groups simply discuss the video and leave the journaling and other content for use outside the gathering. Other groups work their way through each portion together, reading the passages aloud. Again, it's entirely up to your discretion.

As you can see, we have provided Review and Discussion Questions to help spur group discussion.

Each video is roughly fifteen to twenty minutes long. This means it would be possible to do two lessons in one session if necessary. That said, we try to leave as much time for group discussion as possible.

Finally, don't forget this study is just one of many within the Science of Sainthood.

To see more group and individual courses or learn about full access to all the Science of Sainthood studies, visit **ScienceOfSainthood.com!**

# Are you in a Group Study But Want to Watch on Your Own, Too?

Enjoy the course on your own time with a great **discount** on a One Year rental of *Liturgy & Life: Unveiling the Mystical Movement of the Mass*.

It's the perfect way to get as much as possible out of this study!

**Scan the QR Code** with your Phone's Camera & Tap the Link!

LESSON ONE

# Welling Up to Eternal Life

## Lesson Introduction

To begin our series, we need to come to the realization that the liturgy is the mechanism by which we are lifted up into the mystery of God. In fact, the *Catechism of the Catholic Church* says the liturgy is the font from which all the power of the Church flows (n. 1074). And this leads us to the understanding that it doesn't find its origin in man. Rather, the ultimate source of liturgy is the Most Holy Trinity.

 **NOW BEGIN THE VIDEO**

## Notes

# What the Saints Say

"The woman here is the type of the Church, not yet justified, but just about to be. And it is a part of the resemblance, that she comes from a foreign people. The Samaritans were foreigners, though they were neighbours; and in like manner the Church was to come from the Gentiles, and to be alien from the Jewish race." [1]

ST. AUGUSTINE — *5th Century Bishop of Hippo & Doctor of the Church*

[1]Thomas Aquinas, *Catena Aurea: Commentary on the Four Gospels, Collected out of the Works of the Fathers: St. John, ed. John Henry Newman, vol. 4* (Oxford: John Henry Parker, 1845), 139.

# Lectio Divina

"Just then his disciples came. They marveled that he was talking with a woman, but none said, 'What do you wish?' or, 'Why are you talking with her?' So the woman left her water jar, and went away into the city, and said to the people, 'Come, see a man who told me all that I ever did. Can this be the Christ?' They went out of the city and were coming to him.

Meanwhile the disciples besought him, saying, 'Rabbi, eat.'

But he said to them, 'I have food to eat of which you do not know.'

So the disciples said to one another, 'Has any one brought him food?'

Jesus said to them, 'My food is to do the will of him who sent me, and to accomplish his work. Do you not say, "There are yet four months, then comes the harvest?" I tell you, lift up your eyes, and see how the fields are already white for harvest. He who reaps receives wages, and gathers fruit for eternal life, so that sower and reaper may rejoice together. For here the saying holds true, "One sows and another reaps." I sent you to reap that for which you did not labor; others have labored, and you have entered into their labor.'"

JOHN 4:27–38

# Meditation

Many modern readers of this passage fail to understand how shocking it would have been for someone to see Jesus speaking to the woman at the well. The Jews considered the Samaritans to be unclean because of their mixed ancestry and religious syncretism. They descended from the people of northern Israel who were conquered by the Assyrians in 722 BC.

In order to prevent future rebellion, the Assyrians removed mass numbers of conquered Israelites and repopulated the area with foreigners brought in from the far corners of the world. The Israelites left behind eventually intermarried with these non-Israelites and became known as the Samaritans.

And not only did the Jews consider Samaritans unclean, men did not ordinarily interact with women in public who were not members of their family or kinship group. That's why we read that "his disciples returned and were surprised to find him talking with a woman" (John 4:27). To be sure, none of them would have dreamed of doing what Christ did.

But this is a great lesson for baptized members of the Mystical Body of Christ, members of the "New Israel", the Church. Christ's actions are our blueprint. If we're going to be like him, we can't stay within the walls of our churches. We can't simply go to Mass and not share what we have. The grace we receive in the sacraments is meant to empower us to spread the truth, beauty, and goodness of the Catholic faith. We're filled with the "living water" so that we can help Christ pour it out on a parched world.

In other words, "living water" is meant to flow.

As St. Augustine says, "Living water is that which comes out of a spring, in distinction to what is collected in ponds and cisterns from the rain. If spring water too becomes stagnant, i.e. collects into some spot, where it is quite separated from its fountain head, it ceases to be living water." [2]

Similarly, if we remain insular, we'll become stagnant. But we can't let that happen. Souls are at stake and we have an important role in their salvation. As members of Christ's Body, we have to let the living water of his Spirit flow through us to all the "Samaritans" in our world.

[2] Thomas Aquinas, *Catena Aurea: Commentary on the Four Gospels, Collected out of the Works of the Fathers: St. John, ed. John Henry Newman, vol. 4* (Oxford: John Henry Parker, 1845), 141

◆

*"The diverse liturgical traditions have arisen by very reason of the Church's mission... Through the liturgical life of a local church, Christ, the light and salvation of all peoples, is made manifest to the particular people and culture to which that Church is sent and in which she is rooted. The Church is catholic, capable of integrating into her unity, while purifying them, all the authentic riches of cultures."*

———— CCC 1202 ————

# Review Questions

**1.** According to Christ in his conversation with the woman at the well, how do we receive the living water that will quench our thirst for all eternity?

**2.** What does the word "liturgy" mean?

**3.** Where does liturgy ultimately come from? What is its source?

**4.** When did liturgy first appear in human history?

**5.** According to *Sacrosanctum Concilium*—the Second Vatican Council's Constitution on the Liturgy—what document or book is "of the greatest importance in the celebration of the liturgy"?

**6.** Why is going to Mass so important?

# Discussion Questions

**1.** The living water Jesus offers us will quench our inner thirst and satisfy our deepest desires, but as fallen human beings, we often look to other, more worldly sources to satisfy those desires. What are some of those other sources we often turn to? Have any of these other, more worldly sources ever really satisfied you for very long? Why or why not?

**2.** Is the idea that liturgy has its origin in God new to you? Does it change your view of what we do in the Mass? How?

**3.** Take a moment to think about why you go to Mass. Is it just because you have an obligation, or is there a deeper reason? After learning about the meaning and importance of the liturgy, have your reasons for going to Mass changed at all?

**4.** How do Fr. Kavanagh's statements, "I don't go to Mass because I'm Catholic, I'm Catholic because I go to Mass," strike you? Does it reorient your thinking at all?

# Prayer Journal

LESSON TWO

# Shadow, Image, & Reality

---

## What We Covered in Our Last Lesson

In John chapter 4, Jesus encounters a Samaritan woman at a well, and he offers her "living water" that will quench her inner thirst and satisfy her deepest desires. He offers this same living water to each and every one of us, and taking him up on that offer is the goal of this series.

Significantly, soon after Jesus makes this offer to the Samaritan woman, she shifts the topic of conversation to worship. She is concerned with the proper place of worship, but Jesus insists that true worship is not confined to a place. He essentially tells us that if we want this living water that will quench our thirst for all eternity, we have to learn how to worship the Father "in spirit and truth."

What's more, Jesus' offer of living water evokes a number of Old Testament prophecies in books like Ezekiel, Joel, and Isaiah that speak about water in the context of worship. The prophets knew the day was coming when living water would be poured out upon the earth in connection with the worship of God's holy name and saving power, and hundreds of years later, Jesus tells the Samaritan woman that time has come.

Of course, this movement toward the pouring out of living water didn't just begin with the prophets. Liturgical worship of God existed right from the beginning and plays a major role all the way through the story of humanity.

That said, true worship in the New Covenant of Christ consists of far more than simply a modernized version of what we see people doing in ancient times. Christ has come to raise the worship of God's people to its highest and most perfect expression this side of heaven. His gift of living water enables us to worship the Father "in spirit and truth."

And realize that this worship surpasses everything that came before it, even that of the Israelites in the Jerusalem temple. Why? Because the current of this living water is God actually flowing into us and lifting us up to share in his divine life. It elevates us into the supernatural communion of love we call the Trinity. That's the breathtaking power of the living water that flows in and through the liturgical actions of the Church.

So when we say this study is focused upon liturgy, we don't mean that we're simply going to discuss the various parts of the Mass or other forms of liturgy. Certainly that's all important. But we're going beyond the externals, beyond rubrics and rituals, beyond vessels and vestments. We're going to explore the deeper, mystical realities that unite us to Christ and allow us to participate in the divine nature of God.

We're also going to look at where the liturgy leads us. After all, it's designed to move us into a mind-boggling participation in the divine nature of God, a gift so ridiculously incredible that even the most eloquent descriptions fall to the floor as mere stammering and stuttering.

Practically speaking, we're going to look at the liturgy through the lens of Scripture so that we can discover the inner reality that lies hidden beneath the outward signs. Salvation history—the story told in Scripture—is in many ways all about our salvation through liturgy. In fact, you could say the Bible is a liturgical book. It's the Word of God that helps us understand more deeply how to give him proper worship.

Of course, the Bible doesn't read itself. Thankfully, Church teaching helps us to draw out the truth of Scripture, as well as lay some foundation as we begin our study. Drawing upon Scripture, the *Catechism of the Catholic Church* says that "The word 'liturgy' originally meant a 'public work' or a 'service in the name of/on behalf of the people.' In Christian tradition it means the participation of the People of God in 'the work of God.' Through the liturgy Christ, our redeemer and high priest, continues the work of our redemption in, with, and through his Church" (CCC 1069).

This means that liturgy doesn't originate with us. It's "on behalf" of us. It's our "participation" in "the work of God." In other words, we don't just trace what we do as Catholics to ancient biblical times. Authentic liturgy flows from the Holy Trinity, which means we actually trace it all the way back to God.

Pope Pius XII spells this out in his encyclical *Mediator Dei*. "The sacred liturgy is... the public worship which our Redeemer as Head of the Church renders to the Father, as well as the worship which the community of the faithful renders to its Founder, and through Him to the heavenly Father" (n. 20). Simply put, Jesus enables us to do in liturgy what he never ceases to do in eternity—pour out our lives to the Father in love. And understanding this helps us to see more clearly the underlying purpose of the liturgy.

It also helps us to understand more deeply the role of Scripture. The Bible is basically the story of our creation through God's love, how we fell into sin, how God saves us, and that salvation is communicated to us in the liturgy.

# Lesson Introduction

Drawing from the Church Fathers, Cardinal Joseph Ratzinger (i.e. Pope Benedict XVI) identifies three stages of liturgy described in Scripture. They're extremely important to understand because they show us the origin of liturgical worship in human history, what we're doing now and why, and where it's all headed.

**NOW BEGIN THE VIDEO**

# Notes

# What the Saints Say

"The Eucharist not only provides the interior strength needed for this mission, but is also—in some sense—its plan. For the Eucharist is a mode of being, which passes from Jesus into each Christian, through whose testimony it is meant to spread throughout society and culture.

For this to happen, each member of the faithful must assimilate, through personal and communal meditation, the values which the Eucharist expresses, the attitudes it inspires, the resolutions to which it gives rise."

POPE ST. JOHN PAUL II — *Mane Nobiscum Domine n. 25*

# Lectio Divina

"After this I looked, and lo, in heaven an open door! And the first voice, which I had heard speaking to me like a trumpet, said, 'Come up hither, and I will show you what must take place after this.' At once I was in the Spirit, and lo, a throne stood in heaven, with one seated on the throne!

And he who sat there appeared like jasper and carnelian, and round the throne was a rainbow that looked like an emerald. Round the throne were twenty-four thrones, and seated on the thrones were twenty-four elders, clad in white garments, with golden crowns upon their heads. From the throne issue flashes of lightning, and voices and peals of thunder, and before the throne burn seven torches of fire, which are the seven spirits of God; and before the throne there is as it were a sea of glass, like crystal.

And round the throne, on each side of the throne, are four living creatures, full of eyes in front and behind: the first living creature like a lion, the second living creature like an ox, the third living creature with the face of a man, and the fourth living creature like a flying eagle. And the four living creatures, each of them with six wings, are full of eyes all round and within, and day and night they never cease to sing,

'Holy, holy, holy, is the Lord God Almighty,
who was and is and is to come!'"

REVELATION 4:1–8

# Meditation

If the Mass is truly a foretaste of heaven, and we are participants in the holy sacrifice being offered, then it stands to reason that we are supposed to be a foretaste of heaven for others, as well. Empowered by the Eucharist, we are to be "little Christs" in the world, sharing his sacrificial love with those around us. The Mass fills us up with God; it divinizes us so that we can go out and help the Lord divinize all of creation.

Think of yourself as an icon. Icons are not merely pieces of art. Artists don't "paint" an icon, they "write" it. It's theology expressed in sacred images. It's a window into eternity, a peek into paradise.

Filled to the brim with divine life, you and I have become icons of Christ. The Word has been written upon our hearts. We're "living theology" in the midst of a world that desperately needs hope and joy. We should never hide the great gift Christ has given us. People need to be able to see Our Lord in the way we live every aspect of our lives and be a channel through which the Lord can draw others to him.

And while Holy Mass is a sacramental re-presentation of the sacrifice of Christ, never forget that the liturgy doesn't simply end after the closing prayers and recessional. The beauty and grace of Christ walk out the doors of the church in us. They move through us. They make us walking signs of the heavenly realities we just celebrated.

"Our body is a cenacle," says St. Gianna Beretta Molla, "a monstrance: through its crystal the world should see God."

———————————◆———————————

*"In the earthly liturgy we share in a foretaste of that heavenly liturgy which is celebrated in the Holy City of Jerusalem toward which we journey as pilgrims, where Christ is sitting at the right hand of God, Minister of the sanctuary and of the true tabernacle. With all the warriors of the heavenly army we sing a hymn of glory to the Lord; venerating the memory of the saints, we hope for some part and fellowship with them; we eagerly await the Savior, our Lord Jesus Christ, until he, our life, shall appear and we too will appear with him in glory."*

——————————— CCC 1090 ———————————

# Review Questions

**1.** Cardinal Joseph Ratzinger (who eventually became Pope Benedict XVI), taking his cue from the Church Fathers, taught that there are three main stages in humanity's liturgical history. What is the first stage?

**2.** What did Cardinal Ratzinger say was the second stage of humanity's liturgical history?

**3.** What parts of the Mass are unchangeable?

**4.** What are two reasons why some parts of the Mass have changed over time?

**5.** Who has the authority to change and determine the norms for liturgical worship?

# Discussion Questions

**1.** Does it surprise you to learn that the Mass has changed many times over the last two thousand years? Why or why not?

**2.** Does the connection between the ancient liturgical worship we read about in Scripture—the shadow stage—and what we do now in the image stage help you to understand more deeply why we worship the way we do?

**3.** Liturgy isn't just something we do on earth. It's a constant in heaven as well, as shown by the presence of liturgical prayers like the Sanctus, the Alleluia, and the Gloria in the book of Revelation. Have you ever stopped to think about the fact that in the Mass you're actually participating in the worship of the angels and saints in heaven? Does that make you think differently about how you say the responses, pray the prayers, or sing the songs?

**4.** Given a deeper understanding that the Mass is a foretaste of heaven, a real contact point between the human and the divine, has your desire for attending Mass increased? Why or why not?

# Prayer Journal

LESSON THREE

# Giving & Receiving

## What We Covered In Our Last Lesson

Why does God work through liturgy? While we'll have more to say on this later, the simple answer is that liturgy is a reflection of who he is. It's a giving and receiving of love that draws us into the giving and receiving of love among the three Persons of the Trinity.

And we see this liturgical life of God play out in the created world. That's why you find liturgy from front to back in the Bible; from Old Testament blessings, temple offerings, and sacrifices to the New Testament sacrifice of Jesus Christ, and on to the Book of Revelation. And what this tells us is that God created us to be liturgical. Why? Because we're made to enter into the heavenly, Trinitarian liturgy.

But our entrance into the heavenly liturgy isn't something that simply happens later. Our earthly liturgy is already beginning to raise us into the life of God. And it's been moving in this direction from the beginning.

In fact, if we were to zoom out on human history, we would see there are three overall stages of how we can categorize the past, present, and future, so to speak, of liturgy. Drawing from the book of Hebrews chapter 10 and the Church Fathers, Cardinal Joseph Ratzinger describes these stages as shadow, image, and reality.

The first, or shadow, stage is essentially the Old Testament—the time of animal sacrifices, grain offerings, and temple liturgies.

Stage two, the image stage, begins when Jesus Christ, "the image of the invisible God," institutes the central New Testament liturgy at the Last Supper. This new liturgy transforms and surpasses the Old Testament liturgies. Instead of sacrificial animals in a stone temple, we now re-present the once and for all sacrifice of Jesus Christ, consuming the resurrected Lamb of God in the liturgy of the Church.

Ratzinger also says that in this current "image stage", there's a sense in which the liturgy we celebrate, particularly in the Eucharist, is a melding of all three stages of fulfillment. It includes shadow, image, and reality because the Mass is a transformation of the Old Testament liturgy as well as a foretaste of the heavenly reality in the here and now.

So the Mass isn't just another sacrifice like those in the Old Testament. And while our earthly Eucharistic liturgy is a foretaste of heaven, the heavenly reality remains veiled. We can't see it directly or experience it with our senses.

Yes, we still receive the fullness of the Body, Blood, Soul, and Divinity of Christ through the sacramental signs of bread and wine, but it's a veiled reality that points forward to the unveiled reality of what is to come. Looking at a consecrated Host is not the same thing as the Beatific Vision of God in heaven. As St. Paul says, "Now we see in a mirror dimly, but then face to face. Now I know in part; then I shall understand fully, even as I have been fully understood" (1 Corinthians 13:12).

In other words, the Mass is a kind of contact point between the human and the divine. And this brings up a very important issue—namely, the fact that some parts of the Mass are changeable and others are not. Why? The answer is that some parts of the Mass change and others don't for the simple reason that some parts are more "human" than divine. By "human" we mean the Church—operating under divine authority—makes adaptations as she sees fit.

Pope St. John Paul II wrote about this in his Apostolic Letter *Vicesimus Quintus Annus*. He said, "In the Liturgy, and notably that of the sacraments, there is a part which is unchangeable, because it is of divine institution, and of which the Church is the guardian. There are also parts open to change, which the Church has the power and on occasion also the duty to adapt to the cultures of recently evangelized peoples."

So for example, the words of consecration, which are the words of Christ, can't change because they were divinely instituted. They're the words spoken by *the* Word, Jesus Christ, and they bridge the gap between heaven and earth.

On the flipside, we see lots of adaptations over time when it comes to the changeable parts of the Mass. For instance, in the 7th century, Pope St. Gregory the Great moved the position of the Our Father in the Mass to where it now resides. Similarly, the Agnus Dei, or "Lamb of God," wasn't even part of the Roman Rite until Pope Sergius I added it in the seventh century.

But why exactly does the liturgy change over time under the guidance of the Church? For one thing, the Mass has developed as doctrine has developed. The depth of our understanding of the truths of God affects the manner in which we worship God.

Another reason that certain parts of the liturgy change over time is that people and cultures change. As a result, the changeable parts of the Mass adapt so as to evangelize them. As St. John Paul II explained, "The Gospel lives in conversation with the culture, and if the Church holds back from the culture, the Gospel itself falls silent."

That's why Pope St. Gregory the Great instructed the missionary St. Augustine of Canterbury to "use the liturgical customs of the local Churches as you see fit so as to help the people understand the Gospel."[1]

That said, "No sacramental rite may be modified or manipulated at the will of the minister or the community" (CCC 1125). In other words, we can't make the Mass what we want it to be. It comes to us from God through the authority of the Church. And this idea regarding broader Church authority applies to different rites within the Church, as well. While we might individually prefer one rite to another, we can't forget that the same Church that Christ entrusted with the original deposit of faith and that has determined the norms for liturgical worship for 2000 years is the same Church we have now. It wields the authority of Christ in matters that pertain to Christian worship.

As the Vatican II constitution on the liturgy says, "Regulation of the sacred liturgy depends solely on the authority of the Church, that is, on the Apostolic See and, as laws may determine, on the bishop" (SC 22.1). Put simply, the Church has authority over the Church's liturgy.

[1] Venerable Bede's *A History of the English Church and People*, Ch XXVII

# Lesson Introduction

Everything we possess, we have received from God—everything. And while he has lavished us with many gifts, his greatest gift is himself, particularly through the sacramental liturgy.

And what does he want of us? What is he asking of us? He wants us to imitate him. He wants us to receive him and then give ourselves back to him. That's what Catholic life is all about.

 **NOW BEGIN THE VIDEO**

# Notes

<br><br><br><br><br><br><br><br>

# What the Saints Say

"He, therefore, who is not illumined by such great splendor of created things is blind; he who is not awakened by such great clamor is deaf; he who does not praise God because of all these effects is dumb; he who does not note the First Principle from such great signs is foolish.

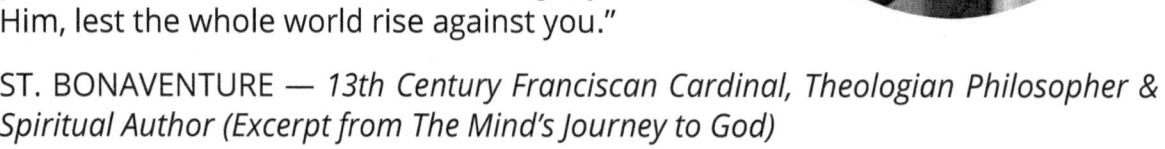

Open your eyes therefore, prick up your spiritual ears, open your lips, and apply your heart, that you may see your God in all creatures, may hear Him, praise Him, love and adore Him, magnify and honor Him, lest the whole world rise against you."

ST. BONAVENTURE — *13th Century Franciscan Cardinal, Theologian Philosopher & Spiritual Author (Excerpt from The Mind's Journey to God)*

# Lectio Divina

"Then the Lord answered Job out of the whirlwind...

'Where were you when I laid the foundation of the earth?
    Tell me, if you have understanding.

Who determined its measurements—surely you know!
   Or who stretched the line upon it?
On what were its bases sunk,
   or who laid its cornerstone,
when the morning stars sang together,
   and all the sons of God shouted for joy?

'Or who shut in the sea with doors,
   when it burst forth from the womb;
when I made clouds its garment,
   and thick darkness its swaddling band,
and prescribed bounds for it,
   and set bars and doors,
and said, 'Thus far shall you come, and no farther,
   and here shall your proud waves be stayed'?"

JOB 38:1, 4–11

# Meditation

Adam and Eve didn't die physically immediately after their sin in the Garden of Eden. But they did die spiritually. They lost the divine life God had given them and were forced to leave his presence. They moved out of Eden and into a kind of private Hades.

And as liturgical theologian Dr. David Fagerberg points out, "Hades comes from a+idean, which means 'invisible'...In Hades, people are deprived of the vision of God, and in the Fall, Adam and Eve wanted to make themselves invisible to God." [1]

But in the liturgy we experience the reverse. Instead of running and hiding, we present ourselves to God. We step out into the open and "present [our] bodies as a living sacrifice, holy and acceptable to God" (Romans 12:1).

And the liturgy doesn't just make us seen by God. It helps us begin to see with the eyes of Christ himself. He fills us with his life and light, so that we can see creation as God sees it. We begin to encounter the entire world through the gaze of eternal love; the love that conquers even death.

[1] Fagerburg, Dr. David, *Liturgical Dogmatics* (San Francisco: Ignatius Press). 2021 p. 142

———————————————— ◆ ————————————————

*"The dual dimension of the Christian liturgy as a response of faith and love*

*to the spiritual blessings the Father bestows on us is thus evident. On the one hand, the Church, united with her Lord and 'in the Holy Spirit,' blesses the Father 'for his inexpressible gift' in her adoration, praise, and thanksgiving. On the other hand, until the consummation of God's plan, the Church never ceases to present to the Father the offering of his own gifts and to beg him to send the Holy Spirit upon that offering, upon herself, upon the faithful, and upon the whole world...."*

———————————————— CCC 1083 ————————————————

# Review Questions

**1.** Why did God create the world? What motivated him?

**2.** When God gives himself to us, what does he ask in return?

**3.** Is the idea of worship as giving and receiving just a Catholic concept?

**4.** What is the only creature on earth that can receive God's gift of himself and return it?

**5.** Why is serving ourselves or worshiping someone or something other than God at the heart of all sin?

**6.** What does the Old Testament seem to indicate is lacking in the realm of the dead?

# Discussion Questions

**1.** God wants us to give our entire selves to him, but in our fallen state, we often want to hold a few things back. Can you think of particular areas of your life that you still haven't fully given over to God? If so, what's keeping you from a more complete surrender to God?

**2.** In our discussion of the sin of Adam and Eve as a failure to worship, we said that "all of our human life and our service to God is a kind of liturgy." In other words, after receiving his love, we're supposed to return it back to him in everything we do. So liturgy isn't just something we do for an hour a week at Mass; it's something that encompasses every part of life.

Does this understanding change your view of the ordinary, seemingly unimportant tasks that often make up our day-to-day life? Practically speaking, how can we make these ordinary tasks part of our worship of God?

**3.** Even though sin can take many forms, at its core it's serving ourselves or the worship of something or someone other than God. In other words, it's an affront primarily to God. Does this knowledge change your attitude toward seemingly "little" sins?

**4.** Every time we sin, we turn away from God and seek fulfillment in lesser things. And much of the healing of the damage wrought by our sin takes place when we turn back to and worship the one true God, which liturgy trains us to do.

Will the fact that the healing of sin happens powerfully through worship change how you participate in the Mass going forward? If so, how? Is there a particular part of the Mass that often strikes you deeply and makes you aware of his healing love and mercy?

# Prayer Journal

LESSON FOUR

# The Exodus Out of Self

---

## What We Covered In Our Last Lesson

All the worship we encounter in the Bible—all the rubrics, rules, regulations and such—aren't random. They were designed by God to bring us into union with him, into union with his self-sacrificial love. And one of the implications of this is that we can't simply make up our own liturgy.

Yes, certain elements of the liturgical celebration can change, but the Church follows the old Latin maxim *lex orandi, lex credendi*—"the law of prayer is the law of faith." In other words, the faith is embedded in the liturgy and practiced through liturgy. Through the Church, God reveals who he is and how we are to receive and respond to him.

And this idea of receiving is extremely important. Everything we possess we have received from God. And the most important thing he gives us isn't a "thing" at all. It's himself, especially through the sacramental liturgy. And in return, he wants us to give ourselves back to him. That's really what the Catholic life is all about.

And this movement of giving and receiving is at the very heart of the relationship of the Trinity. It's the movement of divine love between the Three Persons. The Father gives himself to the Son, the Son gives himself back to the Father, and from this mutual self-donation proceeds a third Person, the Holy Spirit.

And because giving and receiving is at the heart of the Trinitarian life, it's part of us as well. It's built in to who we are. Remember, God made us in his image. He made us to be united with his self-giving family, so the need to give and receive is hard-coded into human DNA.

This idea of giving and receiving even permeates non-Christian religions. In his classic work *The Spirit of the Liturgy,* Joseph Cardinal Ratzinger (Pope Benedict XVI) says that in ancient pagan religions—and even more modern ones—the idea of worship was seen as a kind of circular movement, a kind of giving and receiving.

The gods would sustain the world through their power while the people would feed and sustain the gods through their worship and sacrifices. And this need to give and receive shows that we aren't simply passive observers. We have a role in this world. But it's not to feed God. It's to give him worship. And not because he needs it, but because we do.

In fact, you can see all of this in the creation account in Genesis, says Ratzinger. When God creates, nothing is distinguished as sacred or profane because everything is sacred. It's all a giving of himself by God. And yet—and this is key— it's a gift that awaits acceptance by someone on the other end.

And the only bodily creature on earth that can receive this gift and give it back to God is man, the only one made in his image. And once you start to see the creation of man in this way—as a giving and receiving—some new light is shed on the nature of what actually went wrong in the Garden of Eden.

Made in the image and likeness of a self-giving God, Adam and Eve were supposed to do the same thing he does. They were supposed to receive the life and love offered by the Lord and then give it back to him. But they refused to give him the one thing he asked in return—their obedient love.

Through disobedience, they elevated self-love over love of God, and they began to serve themselves, to worship themselves, instead of God. And there's a sense in which this idolatry, this serving and worshipping something or someone other than God is at the heart of all sin.

Yes, sin might take the form of wronging another person or turning in on ourselves, but at the end of the day, it's primarily an affront to God. We've chosen something else as a greater good than the Lord, and we've set our eyes upon it instead of God.

In light of this, the vital importance of liturgy begins to come into focus. If sin is the worship of something other than God, then in some manner our healing must come through the worship of the true God. After all, if worship is where our problem lies, then worship is where our solution is found.

# Lesson Introduction

In our last lesson we discussed how God gives himself to us and we give ourselves back to him. It's the reciprocal movement of the spiritual life, which takes ritual and sacramental form in the Mass.

But we have a problem. Original Sin has made us captives to the power of sin right out of the box. So how can we become free from this bondage so as to fully give ourselves back to God?

In this lesson we're going to focus on how right from the beginning, sacrificial worship played a pivotal role in setting us free from sin and how the sacrificial system of the Old Testament prepared the way for the sacrifice of the Mass.

## NOW BEGIN THE VIDEO

# Notes

# What the Saints Say

"Let us remember that love lives through sacrifice and is nourished by giving. Let's remember that not everything which is good and beautiful pertains to genuine, essential love, because even without those other things love can be present, indeed a perfected love.

Without sacrifice there is no love. Sacrifice the senses, taste, hearing, and above all, the mind and the will in holy obedience. I wish for you and for myself the best appreciation of sacrifice which is the unconditional willingness to sacrifice."

SAINT MAXIMILIAN KOLBE — *20th Century Saint & Martyr who died in the Auschwitz death camp. (Letter to Fr. Konstanty)*

# Lectio Divina

"For since the law has but a shadow of the good things to come instead of the true form of these realities, it can never, by the same sacrifices which are continually offered year after year, make perfect those who draw near. Otherwise, would they not have ceased to be offered? If the worshipers had once been cleansed, they would no longer have any consciousness of sin. But in these sacrifices there is a reminder of sin year after year. For it is impossible that the blood of bulls and goats should take away sins.

Consequently, when Christ came into the world, he said,

'Sacrifices and offerings thou hast not desired,
 but a body hast thou prepared for me;

in burnt offerings and sin offerings
 thou hast taken no pleasure.

Then I said, "Lo, I have come to do thy will, O God,"
 as it is written of me in the roll of the book.'

When he said above, 'Thou hast neither desired nor taken pleasure in sacrifices and offerings and burnt offerings and sin offerings' (these are offered according to the law), then he added, 'Lo, I have come to do thy will.' He abolishes the first in order to establish the second. And by that will we have been sanctified through the offering of the body of Jesus Christ once for all."

HEBREWS 10:1–10

# Meditation

Worship is not just something we do. It's the end goal of everything. In fact, the entire point of creation is the worship of God.

Pope Benedict XVI says that St. Paul, in the book of Romans, "speaks of the cosmic liturgy, in which the human world itself must become worship of God, an oblation in the Holy Spirit. When the world in all its parts has become a liturgy of God, when, in its reality, it has become adoration, then it will have reached its goal and will be safe and sound."[1]

In other words, worship of God is supposed to be happening at all times and in all places.

And what this tells us is that liturgy isn't something solely performed through the Church's rites and rituals. Our worship of the Lord has to extend into every corner of our lives. We need to face the altar of God and orient ourselves to him in every aspect of our existence.

Put simply, there can be no separation of our lives into compartments. Strictly speaking, there is literally no such thing as a "Sunday Catholic." Even when we are not actively worshiping, all of our activities should ultimately be a sacrifice of love to the Father, Son, and Holy Spirit.

[1] Twomey, Fr. Vincent, *The Dynamics of Liturgy*. (Ignatius Press: San Francisco) 2022, Pg. 58

◆

*"The more one does what is good, the freer one becomes. There is no true freedom except in the service of what is good and just. The choice to disobey and do evil is an abuse of freedom and leads to 'the slavery of sin.'"*

CCC 1733

# Review Questions

**1.** Is sacrifice only a Catholic idea?

**2.** What does exterior sacrifice teach us to do?

**3.** According to the Vatican II document *Gaudium et Spes*, what is the only way we can truly find ourselves?

**4.** What kind of freedom did God want for the Israelites in the Exodus from Egypt?

**5.** While the animal and grain sacrifices in the Old Testament certainly "cost" the Israelites something, what was God really after?

**6.** As Cardinal Joseph Ratzinger says, many people have a negative view of sacrifice. They think of it as a destruction, a loss that has to be avoided. However, the truth is that sacrifice has a positive value as well. What is that positive value? What does sacrifice help us do?

# Discussion Questions

**1.** Quoting our Lord, the book of Acts says, "'It is more blessed to give than to receive'" (20:35). And at least in part, he says that because when we give of ourselves, we're living according to how we're actually made. We're giving and living like the Most Holy Trinity. Think of a situation in your life when you were able to make a gift of yourself to someone else through time, support, an actual gift, or some other means. How did that affect you or make you feel?

Now think of a situation when you did not give of yourself as you should have. Given what we've discussed in the lesson, would you now try to deal with that situation differently? Why?

**2.** Christ gives himself to us completely even though we reject him daily. Are there people in your life that put up barriers to your love, or that you find difficult to give yourself to? How do you deal with them? How *should* you deal with them?

**3.** God's primary purpose in liberating his people from Egypt was to allow them to worship him by sacrifice, not to help them escape their captors into the Promised Land. What does that tell us about the importance of sacrifice and worship?

Do your own personal circumstances sometimes negatively affect how and when you worship (or don't worship) God? Are there practical steps you can take to make changes?

**4.** The Church gives us particular liturgical seasons like Advent and Lent during which we are called to sacrifice worldly goods so as to be more free to offer ourselves to God. Have you ever tried to sacrifice or give up something on a more regular basis (i.e. outside the traditional seasons of penance)? Why or why not? If you have, what was the result?

# Prayer Journal

LESSON FIVE

# From Sacrifice to Sacrament

## What We Covered In Our Last Lesson

In a previous lesson we discussed the whole idea of giving and receiving. God gives himself to us, and we give ourselves back to him. That's the reciprocal movement of the spiritual life, which takes ritual and sacramental form in the Mass.

Of course, it's a little more complicated than that. Loving God requires us to have the freedom of our will so as to give generously and sacrificially of ourselves. Only when we are free can we love as God loves. Authentic love requires freedom. This means we have to conquer the stubbornness and selfishness that are the result of Original Sin. So how does that happen? How can we become free to give ourselves to God with a generosity that mirrors His eternal love?

Put simply, it happens through obedient sacrificial worship. And this idea of sacrifice isn't particular to the Catholic faith. Cardinal Joseph Ratzinger—before he was Pope Benedict XVI—makes a very interesting statement in his book *The Spirit of the Liturgy*. He says that sacrificial worship is a universal feature of religion. It's everywhere, not just in Catholicism.

For example, when Our Lady of Guadalupe showed up 500 years ago at Tepeyac, it was at a time when the Aztecs were sacrificing up to 80,000 human beings in the dedication of one temple. In more ancient times, the Canaanites would brutally sacrifice live babies to the false god Molech by burning them alive.

But why is sacrifice—both good and bad—so pervasive across time and culture? Basically, it's because human beings are made to be sacrificial. It's hard-coded into our DNA because every single one of us is made to be a member of the self-giving Divine family of God. As the Vatican II document *Gaudium et Spes* declares, "Man... cannot fully find himself except through a sincere gift of self" (GS 24).

But again, man became enslaved by sin after the Fall, so God set in motion a plan to rescue us from its power. It was a plan to restore our freedom to love as he loves, to give as he gives. And this plan starts to come into focus in the story of the Israelites' Exodus from Egypt and worship at Mount Sinai.

As told in the book of Exodus, the Israelites became slaves in Egypt, and after hearing their cries, God sent a man named Moses to rescue them. The whole story essentially revolves around Israel's freedom. But it's a very specific kind of freedom.

God's original request through Moses to Pharaoh wasn't "Let my people go to the Promised Land." It was "Let my people go, that they may serve me in the wilderness" (Exodus 7:16). And significantly, the Hebrew word used here for "serve"—*avad*—has a dual meaning of "work" and "worship." It's a liturgical word associated with priestly activity.

So God wasn't saying he wanted the Israelites to have the freedom to possess their own land and live as an independent nation. Rather, his primary concern was their freedom to worship him despite living in a pagan country. It's not that he wasn't concerned with their exterior lack of freedom. He was just *more* concerned with their *interior* lack of freedom.

Following in the footsteps of Adam, the Israelites—God's "firstborn son" (Exodus 4:22)—had turned away from the worship of the one true God. They had become enslaved to idols like their Egyptian captors, and God wanted to free them from idolatry so they could receive the love he was offering and give it back to him.

And once he freed the Israelites from their external slavery, leading them out of Egypt, he continued his plan to free them from their interior slavery. All the things that take place at Mount Sinai—like the giving of the 10 Commandments and the requirement of animal sacrifices—all of it was about freedom and worship. God was constantly trying to teach the Israelites to take their eyes off the things they placed in front of him, to sacrifice the things they loved more than him, in order to free them from disordered love and refocus their affections on him.

Even so, the animal and grain offerings he mandated couldn't really satisfy for sin. But they were an opportunity for the Israelites to start relearning how to give back the life and love God had given to them. It taught them to begin to give up valuable things they possessed so as to prepare them for a gift of themselves. Those early sacrifices weren't everything God wanted, but they were a start. The real goal was sacrificial, obedient love from his children.

But why ask for these sacrifices in the first place? What was the point of all the stone altars, sacrificial animals, and grain offerings? As St. Thomas explains in his *Treatise on Law* (2nd Part), sacrifice is essentially ritualized self-offering. In other words, exterior sacrifice teaches us what's supposed to happen interiorly. It's like at the end of Lent after you've given up beer or chocolate. By the end of the forty days, you realize you're not enslaved to it anymore. It's lost its grip. Through God's grace, sacrifice frees us from the chains of sin and changes our hearts.

Of course, getting to this point of sacrificial service wasn't easy for the Israelites, and it isn't easy for us. They had their false gods, and we have our own gods we don't want to sacrifice. But that's partly because we have a false view of sacrifice. As Ratzinger points out, we have a tendency to think of sacrifice only in terms of death. It's seen as a destruction or loss, so it has a negative connotation.

In reality, sacrifice is a positive thing. Giving up things we value teaches us to give ourselves. It teaches us to begin to live like God in loving self-donation. And while the sacrifices of the Old Testament were the beginning of our re-learning this truth, it's not until the ultimate sacrifice of love through Jesus Christ that we can truly become like God again. Only through the power of his sacrificial gift can we begin to give proper worship, particularly through the sacrifice offered at Holy Mass.

# Lesson Introduction

In our last lesson we began to unpack the essential meaning of sacrifice, particularly in the Old Testament.

In this lesson, we'll discuss more deeply how the notion of sacrifice comes to fulfillment through Jesus Christ and his institution of the Eucharist. In other words, we'll learn more about why God did what he did so as to shed some light on the bigger picture of God's plan for our salvation and see where that plan plays out most powerfully today.

 **NOW BEGIN THE VIDEO**

# Notes

# What the Saints Say

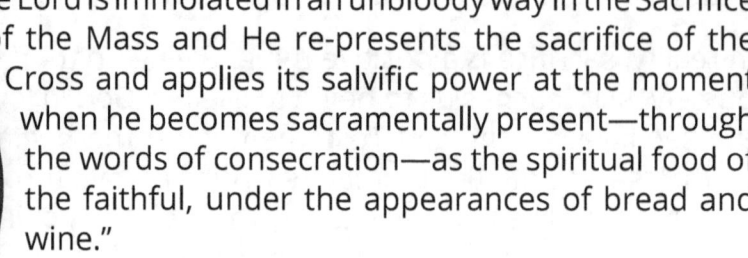

"The Lord is immolated in an unbloody way in the Sacrifice of the Mass and He re-presents the sacrifice of the Cross and applies its salvific power at the moment when he becomes sacramentally present—through the words of consecration—as the spiritual food of the faithful, under the appearances of bread and wine."

POPE ST. PAUL VI — *Mysterium Fidei 35*

# Lectio Divina

"'Has the Lord as great delight in burnt offerings and sacrifices,
   as in obeying the voice of the Lord?
Behold, to obey is better than sacrifice,
   and to hearken than the fat of rams.

For rebellion is as the sin of divination,
   and stubbornness is as iniquity and idolatry.
Because you have rejected the word of the Lord,
   he has also rejected you from being king.'"

1 SAMUEL 15:22–23

# Meditation

As we discussed in the video lesson, when talking about the plan of salvation, it's a mistake to focus only on our freedom from sin. While obviously damaging, sin was merely an obstacle. It needed to be dealt with, but paying the debt of our offenses against God was never the end goal.

From the very beginning, God was after so much more. Or, to put it more appropriately, God was offering so much more. He was (and is) offering an ecstatic eternity through Jesus Christ.

But while sin and its effects tend to dominate and cloud our view in the early years of the spiritual life, over time our gaze begins to focus more on the horizon of heaven. As we mature, we begin to elevate our view and focus more on Christ instead of ourselves.

In fact, we could say that the liturgy—particularly the Mass—is a kind of template of the overall spiritual life. Through it, we both beg (and receive) forgiveness from our Lord for all the wrongs we have committed, as well as begin to receive the promised prize of divine life.

Of course, it's more than a mere template. It's the very life and power of Christ that propels us toward the final goal of participation in the Divine Family.

And that's why if we want to continue to make spiritual progress, we should make every effort to offer ourselves along with Christ in the sacrifice of the Mass as often, and as fully, as possible.

◆

*"Forming 'as it were, one mystical person' with Christ the head, the Church acts in the sacraments as 'an organically structured priestly community.' Through Baptism and Confirmation the priestly people is enabled to celebrate the liturgy, while those of the faithful 'who have received Holy Orders, are appointed to nourish the Church with the word and grace of God in the name of Christ.'"*

CCC 1119

# Review Questions

**1.** Why does our disobedience to God eventually lead to death?

**2.** We tend to view Jesus' Incarnation, Passion, death, and Resurrection only in terms of past sin, but dealing with the failure of Adam and Eve wasn't the final goal of Christ.  What was God's original and primary goal for humanity?

**3.** What is the mechanism that now allows us to participate in God's family life?

**4.** Are ordained bishops and priests the only priests in the Church?

**5.** What is the role of the laity at Mass?

# Discussion Questions

**1.** Jesus doesn't just save us *from* something—sin and death. He also saves us *for* something—divine life. He brings us into future glory, into the self-giving family of God. Does that perspective alter your view of what's ultimately happening at Mass? Does the teaching that we receive the Body, Blood, Soul and Divinity of Christ in the Eucharist now take on a new meaning?

**2.** As discussed by Matthew in the lesson, we are called to participate in the sacrifice of Mass, to "present our bodies as a living sacrifice", in the words of St. Paul. Does the idea of offering yourself as a sacrifice along with Christ make you nervous? Why? What do you think we're being called to do on a practical level?

**3.** Have you ever struggled with feeling like a mere spectator at Mass? Did you learn anything from this lesson that would help overcome that feeling?

# Prayer Journal

LESSON SIX

# Preparing to Participate in the Mystery

---

## What We Covered In Our Last Lesson

Even though God used the Old Testament sacrificial system to teach his people to give themselves back to him, just as he gives himself to us, that system wasn't perfect. As the Second Vatican Council document *Dei Verbum* says, it was "provisional and imperfect" (DV 15).

That doesn't mean the provisions laid out by God were bad. Not at all. In fact, they worked pretty well. Among other things, they helped draw the children of Israel away from the worship of idols. Even so, the Old Testament sacrifices and offerings were kind of a low bar, so to speak. By God's design, they were intended to be provisional rather than permanent. In other words, they weren't what he ultimately wanted.

It's kind of like how parents lower their expectations and demands of younger children. When you have a toddler, you first teach them not to throw food off of the highchair and onto the floor, and only when they get older do you ask them to wash their own dishes.

Similarly, God came down to his children's level in order to teach them to grow up. He started with more rudimentary lessons tailored to their abilities, and then increased the requirements later on.

The problem was that we weren't ready to do what he wanted. We always fell short. We were disobedient, and there were consequences for our disobedience—namely, death. You see, disobedience cuts us off from the Giver of life himself. Similar to how a deep sea diver cuts himself off from life by cutting his air hose and dropping his tanks to the ocean floor, serious disobedience cuts us off from God's life-giving love.

To be sure, God never stopped offering us his life and love. We simply rejected his offer over and over again. We needed to learn that loving obedience is the key to life. And that's where Jesus comes into the picture.

We couldn't get out of the mess we put ourselves in. As sinners, we weren't capable of making an offering that would satisfy for our offenses against God.

Nevertheless, divine justice said that satisfaction had to be made for our sin. So in divine mercy, God stepped in and did what we couldn't. God became man and offered himself as a perfectly humble, obedient, loving sacrifice on our behalf.

The human race was represented and redeemed by a flesh-and-blood man who was also God. That's the basic logic of the cross, the basic logic of how we are saved, so to speak.

That said, Christ didn't just save us from sin. The plan wasn't just for us to be forgiven. Rather, the plan was for us to become sons and daughters in the family of God. So Jesus formed a New Covenant—a new family relationship—to allow us to participate in his divine life. Restoring our innocence is only part of the picture; the ultimate goal is divine adoption through a participation in the divine life of the Trinity.

This is really important because all too often we focus only upon what we're saved from and not what we're saved for. We often view Christ's Incarnation, Passion, death and Resurrection only in terms of past sin, but we need to also understand it in terms of the astounding grace he provides in the present moment, as well as our promised future glory. He came to pour himself out upon us in a way so breathtaking that we can barely begin to grasp it.

And that is where the liturgy comes into play. It's the mechanism, so to speak, for how Christ draws us into a real participation in God's family life. It's where Christ's sacrifice becomes the gift of salvation and divine life. Beginning with Baptism and culminating in the Eucharist, we are joined to him, and through him we can offer ourselves back to the Father.

As paragraph 1322 of the Catechism says, "Those who have been raised to the dignity of the royal priesthood by Baptism and configured more deeply to Christ by Confirmation participate with the whole community in the Lord's own sacrifice by means of the Eucharist."

This means that we're not supposed to be mere spectators at Mass. We're invited to be full-on participants with a real and powerful liturgical role and duty. As members of the Mystical Body of Christ—literally joined to him through the sacraments—we are offering ourselves along with his sacrifice, so we can now fully give ourselves back to God in the manner he's always desired. Namely, through obedient, self-sacrificial love.

In fact, Cardinal Joseph Ratzinger even says that our participation in the sacrifice of Christ is necessary for the salvation of the world. Why? Because while Christ's "once for all" (Hebrews 7:27) self-offering was totally perfect and sufficient for our salvation, it's not finished because it's not finished in us.

To put it another way, objectively speaking, the sacrifice of Christ was perfect and all-sufficient for the salvation of the world. There was nothing imperfect or insufficient about it in the least. However, *subjectively* speaking, his sacrifice awaits our participation to have its full effect on the world. That will happen only when we all allow the obedient self-gift of Christ to penetrate us and perfect our worship, to perfect our loving, obedient gift of self to God and neighbor.

# Lesson Introduction

One of the primary ideas in the Second Vatican Council's document on the liturgy revolves around the term "active participation." The problem is that this term is often greatly misunderstood and misapplied. In this lesson we'll discover exactly what active participation means and discover how a deeper understanding of our participation provides us the secret to preparing ourselves for Mass.

 **NOW BEGIN THE VIDEO**

# Notes

# What the Saints Say

"Let the entire man be seized with fear; let the whole world tremble; let heaven exult when Christ, the Son of the Living God, is on the altar in the hands of the priest. O admirable height and stupendous condescension!

O humble sublimity! O sublime humility! that the Lord of the universe, God and the Son of God, so humbles Himself that for our salvation He hides Himself under a morsel of bread. Consider, brothers, the humility of God and 'pour out your hearts before Him', and 'be ye humbled that ye may be exalted by Him.'

Do not therefore keep back anything for yourselves that He may receive you entirely who gives Himself up entirely to you."

ST. FRANCIS OF ASSISI — *13th Century Italian Mystic & Founder of the Franciscans* (*The Writings of St. Francis of Assisi*, tr. by Paschal Robinson, [1905])

# Lectio Divina

"Do you not know that in a race all the runners compete, but only one receives the prize? So run that you may obtain it. Every athlete exercises self-control in all things. They do it to receive a perishable wreath, but we an imperishable.

Well, I do not run aimlessly, I do not box as one beating the air; but I pommel my body and subdue it, lest after preaching to others I myself should be disqualified."

1 CORINTHIANS 9:24–27

# Meditation

In 1 Corinthians chapter 9, St. Paul describes his own ascetical practices saying, "I do not run aimlessly, I do not box as one beating the air; but I pommel my body and subdue it lest after preaching to others I myself should be disqualified" (1 Corinthians 9:26–27).

And the context of why he wrote this to the church in Corinth helps to drive home the point that as human beings made in the image of God, we are a union of body and soul, and that what we do in our bodies makes a lot of difference.

The Corinthians—to put it mildly—were a troubled bunch. To say that there was terrible immorality ravaging the community would be a mild understatement. Among other things, Paul makes reference to their issues with prostitution (1 Corinthians 6:12–20) and even incest (1 Corinthians 5:1–5).

One of the underlying problems in Corinth was the tendency to divide body and soul. They mistakenly thought that Christianity makes its claim on what we believe but not on how we live. It determines our creed, but has nothing to say about our conduct. But that is a serious misunderstanding. As discussed in the lesson, we are a union of body and soul. We aren't pure spirits. How we act with our bodies seriously matters.

That's why Paul told the Corinthians, "The body is not meant for immorality, but for the Lord, and the Lord for the body. And God raised the Lord and will also raise us up by his power. Do you not know that your bodies are members of Christ" (1 Corinthians 6:14–15)?

We can't sin with our body and think it has no effect on our relationship with God. It does. An intrinsic part of our humanity, our body has to be brought into submission along with everything else. The sin of Adam and Eve left us with disordered passions that influence our bodily actions in all kinds of ways.

That's why St. Paul says that he "pommels" and "subdues" his body. He knows that it is directly connected to his interior life. He knows he can't separate his bodily actions from his spirituality, so he disciplines it.

And this is a theme picked up by all the spiritual masters of the Church. As St. John of the Cross wrote, "I should like to persuade spiritual persons that the road leading to God... demands only the one thing necessary: true self-denial, exterior and interior" (*Ascent of Mount Carmel* 2.7.8).

And while self-denial and disciplining our bodies doesn't sound fun, realize that the end result isn't misery. It's freedom. It's not death. It's life! We subdue our bodies because along with our soul, it is being divinized. It is being prepared for resurrection into new life so beautiful we can't even begin to fathom it. (1 Corinthians 2:9)

That's why near the end of his first letter to the Corinthians, St. Paul exhorts his audience to continue to press forward toward a new life that will change everything in the blink of an eye.

"We shall all be changed, in a moment, in the twinkling of an eye, at the last trumpet. For the trumpet will sound, and the dead will be raised imperishable, and we shall be changed. For this perishable nature must put on the imperishable, and this mortal nature must put on immortality. When the perishable puts on the imperishable, and the mortal puts on immortality, then shall come to pass the saying that is written:

"Death is swallowed up in victory."

"O death, where is thy victory?

O death, where is thy sting?"

Therefore, my beloved brethren, be steadfast, immovable, always abounding in the work of the Lord, knowing that in the Lord your labor is not in vain" (1 Corinthians 15:51–58).

———————————————————◆———————————————————

*"The assembly should prepare itself to encounter its Lord and to become 'a people well disposed.' The preparation of hearts is the joint work of the Holy Spirit and the assembly, especially of its ministers. The grace of the Holy Spirit seeks to awaken faith, conversion of heart, and adherence to the Father's will. These dispositions are the precondition both for the reception of other graces conferred in the celebration itself and the fruits of new life which the celebration is intended to produce afterward."*

———————————————— CCC 1098 ————————————————

# Review Questions

**1.** What is the name of the particular thing we're supposed to be doing in the Mass?

**2.** According to Joseph Cardinal Ratzinger (Pope Benedict XVI), what's the central part of Mass in which we're called to participate?

**3.** What effect did the sin of Adam and Eve have on our passions? How did it impact the original harmony of body and soul?

**4.** "To exercise" or "train" in Greek is the little word *askeo*. What word do we get from it and what does it mean?

**5.** According to Fr. Donald Haggerty, how does asceticism help to counter the effects of Original Sin?

**6.** What image from the Old Testament did St. John of the Cross use to teach us about turning our attention from earthly goods to God's heavenly gifts?

**7.** Why is it important to bring our body into the sacrificial action of our spirit through asceticism?

# Discussion Questions

**1.** Had you ever heard of the term "active participation" before this lesson? If so, what did it mean to you?

Has your understanding of what it means to participate been altered by the discussion of our movement into the action of Christ, especially at the moment of consecration?

**2.** Our participation in Christ's offering doesn't end with the recessional. Rather, we're supposed to open ourselves to be filled with the grace of God's presence, and then allow him to overflow into the world through us. Practically speaking, what should this look like in our own lives? What are some concrete ways we can let God's presence within us affect the people around us?

**3.** Before this lesson, had you ever heard that asceticism, in other words, acts of self-denial and bodily penance undertaken to promote spiritual growth, has a role in the spiritual life outside of Lent and Advent? Have you ever tried to practice asceticism outside of these particular liturgical seasons set aside for it? If so, what did you do? What was the result?

Certainly ascetical practices—even minor ones—can present challenges. We don't naturally want to give things up. Does seeing that penances are a powerful way to prepare for Mass help motivate you? Does it make sense that ultimately, penances are an act of love?

**4.** While other Science of Sainthood studies focus more directly on the life of prayer, we need to understand that our conversation with God in prayer plays a vital part in our preparation for Mass, as well as in the Mass itself. As Pope Benedict XVI declared in a 2009 homily, "The Eucharistic Celebration is the greatest and highest act of prayer."

Do you ever spend time in prayer during the week preparing for the great prayer of the Eucharistic Liturgy? If so, what does that look like practically speaking? If not, would you consider spending time with God on a daily basis preparing to receive the gift of the Eucharist?

**5.** St. John Paul II essentially said that we have to possess ourselves before we can give ourselves away. (The exact quote is "Mastery of oneself (self control)... is indispensable that man may be able to 'give himself'" (General Audience, Wednesday, January 16, 1980.)) Ponder his statement for a moment. What does it say about our ultimate calling as humans made in the image of God? Does it help you make even more sense out of sacrifice and asceticism?

# Prayer Journal

# Summary of Lesson Six

In a previous lesson, we talked about how everyone has a role and sacred duty at Mass. As baptized members of the Mystical Body of Christ, all of us are called to offer ourselves along with our Lord back to the Father. In fact, there's a particular term for what we're called to do in the Mass. It's called "active participation," and it's extremely important to understand what this expression means if we're going to encounter God more deeply in the Mass.

While the term has been around since the beginning of the 20th century, it is most closely linked to Vatican II. In *Sacrosanctum Concilium*—one of the four main documents or "Constitutions" of the Second Vatican Council—we read:

"Mother Church earnestly desires that all the faithful should be led to that fully conscious, and active participation in liturgical celebrations which is demanded by the very nature of the liturgy. Such participation by the Christian people as 'a chosen race, a royal priesthood, a holy nation, a redeemed people' (1 Pet. 2:9; cf. 2:4–5), is their right and duty by reason of their baptism" (SC 14).

A lot of discussion has revolved around what "active participation" means, and unfortunately, some people twist its meaning to justify all kinds of extraneous and unnecessary activity surrounding the liturgy. Joseph Cardinal Ratzinger—who was present at Vatican II and later became Pope Benedict XVI—says that active participation has nothing to do with us multiplying activities. Rather, it's about us participating in the one activity of Christ the High Priest.

After hearing and receiving the word of God in faith, the principal action in which we are called to take part, says Ratzinger, is the Eucharistic prayer in the Mass. "The real liturgical action, the true liturgical act," he says, "is the… great prayer that forms the core of the Eucharistic celebration." [1]

In other words, the true center of the Mass and the place where our participation is most fully realized is in the prayer at the consecration. This is where the priest is no longer acting as Father "So and So" speaking as himself on behalf of us. This is where he moves into the first person "I" of Christ, and at this sacred moment, Jesus Christ himself, the Great High Priest of the New Covenant, speaks through his earthly priest to make his sacrifice of salvation present in our midst.

So when we talk about "active participation," we're talking about us participating in the action of Christ on the altar. It's a joining of ourselves to it, to him. Remember, every baptized Christian is a member of the Mystical Body of Christ. And joined to him through the sacraments, we are invited to participate in the offering of Christ our High Priest to the Father as well. His work, his action in the Mass, becomes our work, our action as we join our wills to his and act in unison with him.

This is why the participation we're talking about is something way beyond the externals. Yes, we do things like sing, read, sit, and kneel, but these things are meant to draw us into something even more important. Everything leads to and culminates in the Eucharistic prayer, the moment when Christ re-presents his once-and-for-all sacrifice. And because we are joined to him, we participate, we present ourselves on the same altar as members of his body.

That said, our participation in Christ's offering doesn't end with the recessional. Rather, our participation fills us with Christ's grace and power so that like him, we too can be active at every moment of every day in the world and participate in its redemption. We're supposed to open ourselves to be filled with the grace of God's presence, and then allow him to overflow into the world through us.

But there is another element to all of this discussion of participation and transformation. If we're going to truly participate in the Eucharistic action of Christ in the liturgy, we have to prepare for it. We can't just roll into Mass, tank up on grace, and roll out. We have to bring the rest of the week into play as well.

It's like an athlete preparing for a game or a musician preparing for a concert. They have to practice before the big event, and it's the same with us. If we're going to help transform the world and achieve the glory of heaven, we have to practice as well.

In the spiritual life, that practice involves asceticism, which would normally include things like fasting, abstinence, early prayer, foregoing certain conveniences, etc.. Asceticism is necessary because while God originally made us a harmonious union of body and soul, Original Sin messed things up. We lost full control of ourselves, and our passions became unruly.

To combat those tendencies, we sometimes need to give up good things we like in order to help us gain control of ourselves and acquire the spiritual strength not be ruled by our disordered passions. Remember, we're supposed to be offering ourselves through Christ back to the Father and others, but we can't give away what we don't control.

Paraphrasing St. John Paul II, we have to possess ourselves before we can give ourselves away. In other words, we have to gain control over our whole selves so that we make a gift of our whole selves. That's what asceticism allows. It frees us from being ruled by our passions so we can freely give ourselves in love to others.

That said, your asceticism doesn't have to be "over-the-top". Fast from a meal or two during the week or turn down the hot water at the end of your shower and say a (quick) Hail Mary. There are all kinds of ways we can practice minor acts of self-renunciation that free us from being enslaved to this world so we can make a gift of ourselves.

To be clear, this doesn't mean that the world is bad. On the contrary, God made it for our enjoyment. It's good. But we don't want it to keep us from something better—the self-gift of Christ. Asceticism helps free us from lower things so that we can give ourselves over to higher things.

What we're doing through asceticism is bringing our body into the sacrificial action of our spirit. We are a union of flesh and spirit, body and soul, so we worship God with our whole person, not just our soul. Body and soul form a unity, and both parts have to work in harmony for us to move toward our final union with God.

And remember that the point of all of our asceticism isn't to impose some kind of sacrificial drudgery. Not at all. "Eucharist means first of all 'thanksgiving,'" says the Catechism (CCC 1306).

By preparing for Mass appropriately, we're showing God how much we value it. We're saying "thank you!" for what he's done for us. Small penances are acts of love that tell Our Lord we value him more than these other things.

[1] Ratzinger, Joseph Cardinal, *The Spirit of the Liturgy*. (Ignatius Press: San Francisco) 2000, Pg. 172

# Take the next step!

**Go to ScienceOfSainthood.com today and experience a whole new level of prayer and relationship with God!**

*"Blown away"*

*"I can hardly believe how wonderful this is."*

**Courses in the Science of Sainthood include:**

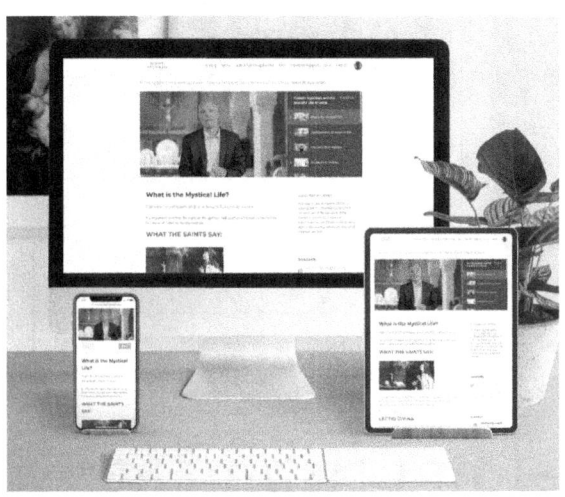

Introduction to Real Prayer

The 7 Deadly Sins

The Moral Virtues

The Theological Virtues

The Dark Night of the Soul

Total Abandonment to God's Will

St. Teresa of Avila's 9 Grades of Prayer

The Gifts of the Spirt ...and more!

*"If you've ever wanted to deepen your life of prayer and actually make some progress in avoiding vice and growing in virtue, then look no further. The Science of Sainthood is for you."*

–**Dr. Brant Pitre**, *Renowned theologian & author of* Jesus and the Jewish Roots of the Eucharist

# ScienceofSainthood.com

**Scan the QR Code** with your Phone's Camera & Tap the Link!

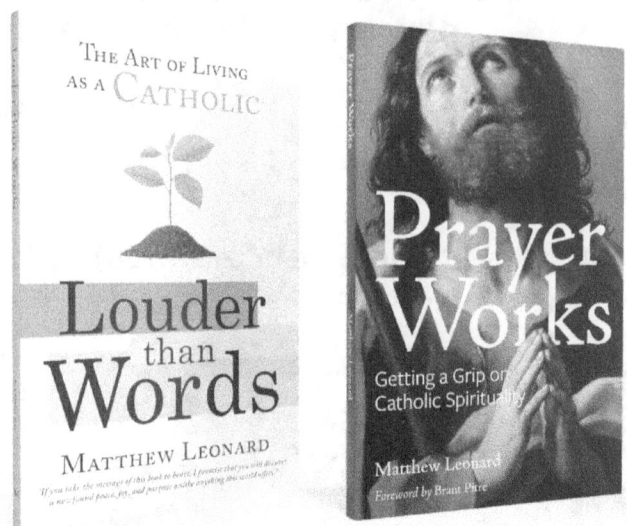

www.ingramcontent.com/pod-product-compliance
Lightning Source LLC
Chambersburg PA
CBHW082007140626

46553CB00020B/2643